Made with Love

How Babies Are Made

For Ben — K.P.

For my talented boyfriend, Endaf — C.M.

First published in 2003 by Macmillan Children's Books
a division of Macmillan Publishers Limited
20 New Wharf Road, London N1 9RR
Basingstoke and Oxford
Associated companies worldwide
www.panmacmillan.com

ISBN 0 333 71679 5 (HB)
ISBN 0 333 74186 2 (PB)

Text copyright © 2003 Kate Petty
Illustrations copyright © 2003 Charlotte Middleton
Moral rights asserted.

1 3 5 7 9 8 6 4 2 (HB)
1 3 5 7 9 8 6 4 2 (PB)

A CIP catalogue record for this book is available
from the British Library.

Printed in Belgium by Proost.

Made with Love

How Babies Are Made

Illustrated by
Charlotte Middleton

Written by
Kate Petty

MACMILLAN
CHILDREN'S BOOKS

"You grew in my tummy. Everyone in the world was once a baby in their mum's tummy."

"How did I get into your tummy?"

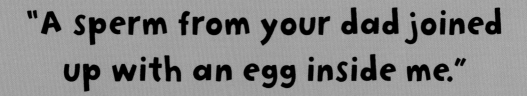

**"A sperm from your dad joined
up with an egg inside me."**

A woman is born with eggs inside her.
A man has sperm.

An egg is smaller than a single grain of sand.
Sperm are much, much smaller than eggs.

"So dads have sperm..."

"And mums have eggs!"

"It happened when your dad and I made love."

When a dad and a mum love each other and want to make a baby, they make love. This is also called having sex.

A mum has a vagina and a dad has a penis.

penis

vagina

The dad and the mum hold each other close so the dad's penis can fit into the mum's vagina. The sperm come out of the penis into the vagina.

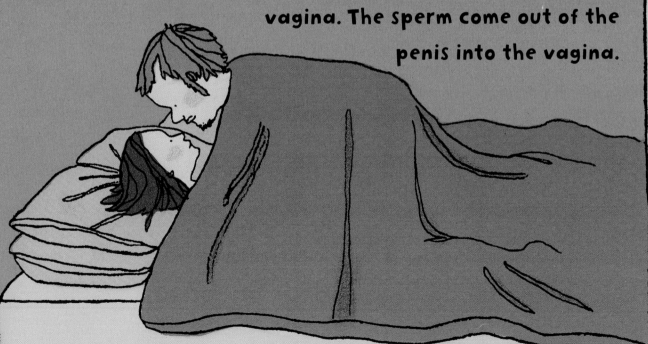

"But how did the sperm and the egg find each other?"

"The sperm swam like tadpoles to the egg."

Millions of sperm race to where the egg
is waiting, but only one sperm gets
to join up with the egg.
This is called "fertilisation".
Sometimes none of the sperm joins up
with the egg, so a baby can't be made.

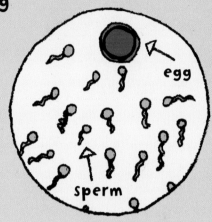

"I wonder if we've made a baby?"

"I hope so."

"As soon as they joined together, the egg began to grow and change into you."

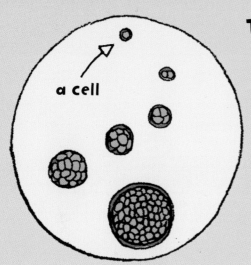

a cell

The fertilised egg starts off as a tiny dot called a "cell". This cell divides into two cells. Then those cells divide again and again until there are millions of cells.

This ball of cells travels to the mum's womb, which is a special place inside her tummy. Inside the mum's womb, the baby floats in a liquid to keep it safe.

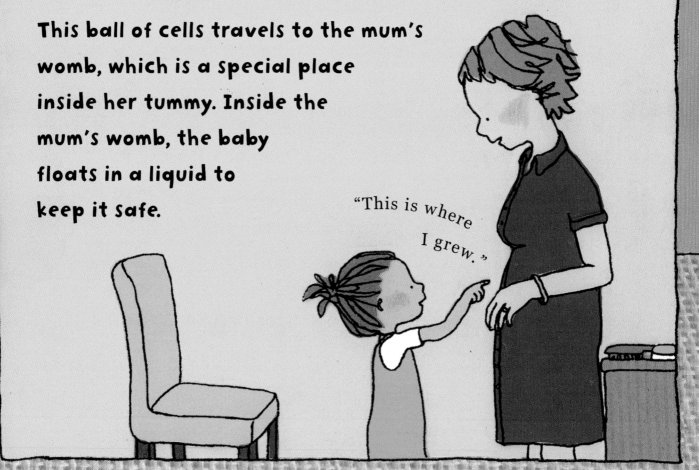

"This is where I grew."

"When did I start to look like a baby?"

"Well, at first you looked more like a little fish than a baby. You even had a tail."

embryo

(larger than life size)

After about four weeks, the ball of cells had turned into a tiny "embryo", about the size of a pea.

This then turned into a baby-shaped "foetus", which grew like this.

Actual size at 10 weeks

at 3 months

at 6 months

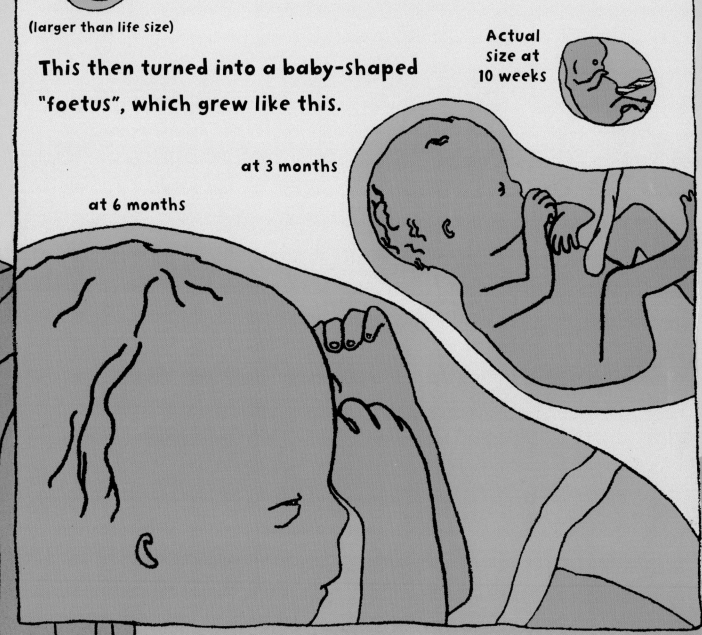

"And was I still in your tummy for all this time?"

"Yes, you stayed there for nine months, and as you grew my tummy got bigger and bigger."

"Could you feel me moving inside you?"

"Yes, I could feel you stretching and kicking."

The baby practises moving. At first it feels like a butterfly fluttering its wings. As the baby gets bigger, the mum feels it turning and squirming.

Sometimes you can even see a big baby move — it makes the mum's tummy move.

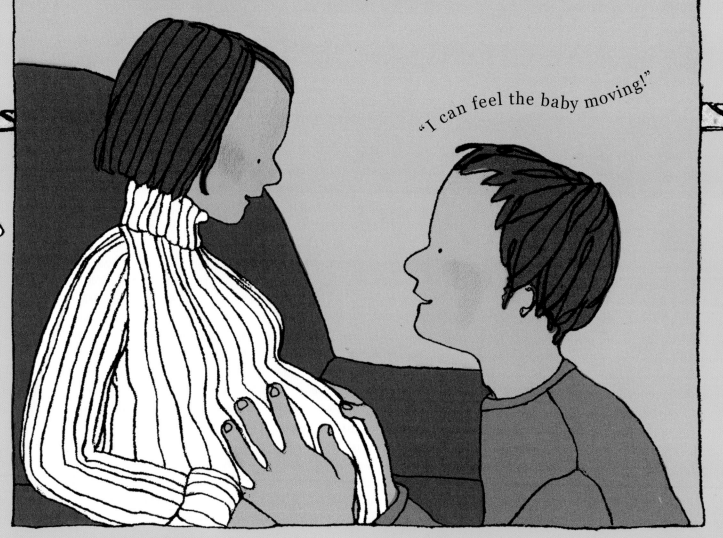

"I can feel the baby moving!"

"What did I eat when I was inside Mum?"

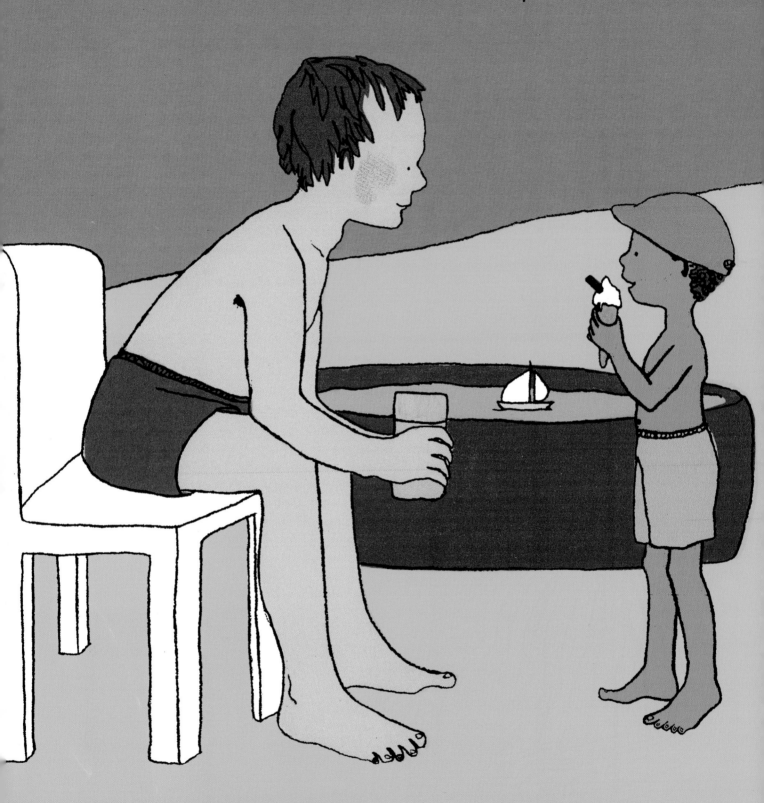

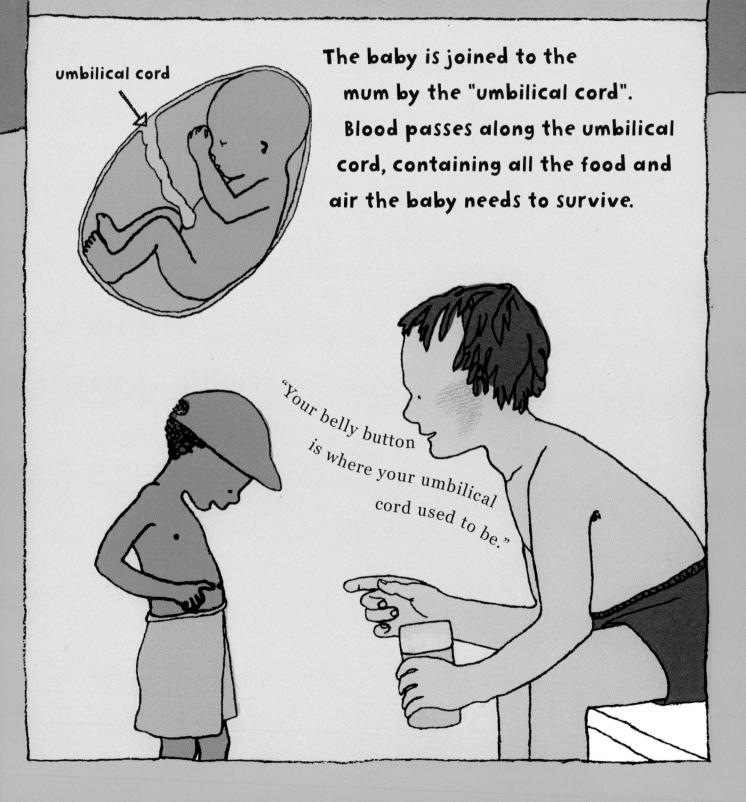

"How did you know when I was
ready to be born?"

"What was the first thing I did
when I was born?"

"The muscles in my body began to push you out."

"Nearly there!"

After nine months a baby is ready to be born.
The mum's muscles work hard to push the baby out
of her womb. Babies usually come out head first.

"You took your first breath and yelled!"

Then I gave you a cuddle and we started
to get to know you.

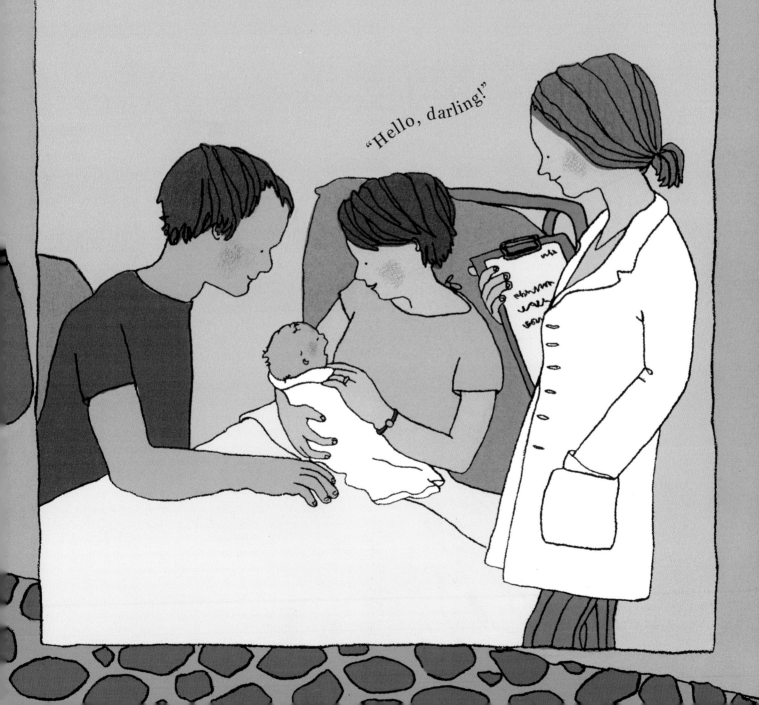